D0515861

History's Mysteries

Perplexing People

Gary L. Blackwood
with Susan Martins Miller

Marshall Cavendish
Benchmark
New York

Marshall Cavendish Benchmark
99 White Plains Road
Tarrytown, NY 10591
www.marshallcavendish.us

Library of Congress Cataloging-in-Publication Data

Blackwood, Gary L.
  Perplexing people / by Gary L. Blackwood with Susan Martins Miller.
    p. cm. — (Benchmark rockets—history's mysteries)
  Includes bibliographical references and index.
  Summary: "Discusses the mysteries surrounding history's most perplexing people"—Provided by publisher.
    ISBN 978-0-7614-4360-5
  1. Impostors and imposture—Biography—Juvenile literature. I. Miller, Susan Martins. II. Title.

CT9980.B57 2009
920.02—dc22
[B]
2008052764

Publisher: Michelle Bisson
Editorial Development and Book Design: Trillium Publishing, Inc.

Photo research by Trillium Publishing, Inc.

Cover photos: Musée Louis XVII/Alexander Kucharsky ou Couaski (Louis-Charles); Centre Historique des Archives Nationales, Paris, AEII 2490 (Joan of Arc)

The photographs and illustrations in this book are used by permission and through the courtesy of: *iStockphoto.com*: Ken Pilon (rectangular frame), front cover, back cover, 1, 3; Eliza Snow (oval frame), front cover, 1. *Musée Louis XVII*: Alexander Kucharsky ou Couaski (Louis-Charles), 1, 14. *Centre Historique des Archives Nationales, Paris*: AEII 2490 (Joan of Arc), 1, 5. *Corbis*: Bettmann, 7, 24. *Library of Congress*: 9, 10, 18, 19. *The Bridgeman Art Library International*: Chateau de Versailles, France/ Lauros/Giraudon, 13. *The Art Archive*: Musée Carnavalet Paris/Gianni Dagli Orti, 17. *Pierre Gilliard*: 21. *The Granger Collection, New York*: 23. *Hamilton County Genealogy Society and Library*: 27.

Printed in Malaysia
1 3 5 6 4 2

Contents

Introduction

This book is about pretenders.

Pretenders make claims about their identity. Sometimes they claim to be long-lost kings or queens. Sometimes they claim to be people everyone thinks are dead.

You might think that the word *pretenders* only means people who pretend to be someone they know they are not. However, some pretenders make claims they really believe are true. They honestly believe they are someone else. Sometimes, other people identify the pretender. These people say they know who the person really is and they want everyone else to know, too.

As time passes, it becomes even harder to be sure of anything about a pretender. Researchers try to solve the mysteries, but records are not always complete. More recently, historians are turning to science. Examining **DNA** evidence sometimes clears up the mystery. However, sometimes DNA only raises more questions.

So how can anyone know the truth? Perhaps we can't. Perhaps the past is a puzzle that even the experts will not solve. This may not be so bad, though, because mysteries keep life interesting. This book opens the door to the mysteries of five pretenders.

CHAPTER ONE

The Maid

Jeanne d'Arc rescued France from the English in the fifteenth century.

In the fifteenth century, a young girl named Jeanne grew up in France in a family called d'Arc. Jeanne d'Arc, also known as Joan of Arc, lived in the village of Domrémy. In her teens, Jeanne began to hear voices saying she would save France from the English. In 1429, Jeanne led an army that freed the city of Orléans. She also won several other important battles. Because she was a young, unmarried woman, people began to call her "the Maid." The next year, the English captured Jeanne and put her on trial for witchcraft. The English found her guilty. The sentence was death. On May 30, 1431, Jeanne d'Arc was burned at the stake.

Or was she?

At her trial, Jeanne was sure she would be saved. Even at the time of the burning, many people believed that the young woman had somehow escaped death.

A witness to the burning said the young woman's face was covered. This would make it hard to be sure who really died. Perhaps someone took Jeanne's place at the last minute. Rumors spread quickly that the Maid was still alive.

Five years later, a woman appeared in the city of Metz. She announced that she was the Maid. Two of the d'Arc brothers came immediately to see this young woman. They believed their sister had died at the time of the **execution**. Now, however, they recognized this young woman as their sister. Some old friends also recognized her.

This young woman married Robert des Armoises. She became known as Jeanne des Armoises. Robert des Armoises clearly called his wife the Maid of France in a land contract. Many people believed the young woman was the same person who had led the army against the English.

In 1439, Jeanne des Armoises visited the city of Orléans. The people of the city held a banquet in her honor. They even gave her money. They believed she was the hero who had freed the city from the English ten years earlier.

One fifteenth century writer said about Jeanne's execution, "They burned her, or another woman like her."

Records show that the next year Madame des Armoises, the same woman who had visited Orléans, arrived in Paris and claimed to be the Maid. After this time, however, historical records do not mention her again.

About the same time, another woman claimed to be the Maid. Her name was Jeanne la Feronne. When she stood before France's King Charles VII in 1440, he believed she was Jeanne d'Arc. Supposedly, she had secret information that only the king and the Maid would know. But later Jeanne la Feronne confessed that she was not the Maid.

Other women also claimed to be Jeanne d'Arc. In 1457, a woman named Jeanne de Sermaize was released from prison. Her crime was that she had called herself the Maid and lied to many people along the way.

Clearly Jeanne des Armoises was the most likely woman to be the Maid. After all, even the brothers of Jeanne d'Arc believed her. If she was the Maid of France, though, how did she escape being burned? She would have needed a lot of help from other people. Someone would have had to be burned in her place. Many people wonder why anyone would go to so much effort to save a peasant girl.

Some scholars suggest that Jeanne d'Arc was not a peasant after all. Instead, she may have been a member of the royal family. She may have been the half sister of King Charles VII. According to this **theory**, King Charles VII's mother, Queen Isabeau, sent the girl away to live with the d'Arc family.

There is no real evidence that Jeanne was the half sister of the king. However, this idea would explain why someone would have wanted to be sure Jeanne, a child of the queen, was not burned at the stake.

CHAPTER TWO

The Mask

A mysterious Frenchman died on November 19, 1703, in prison. No one ever claimed to be him, though. That is because only King **Louis XIV** and his closest advisers knew who the man was. No one else knew what he looked like or what his name was. For hundreds of years, he has been known as "the Man in the Iron Mask." While he was alive, he was called "the unknown prisoner," "the old prisoner," or simply "the Mask."

No one was allowed to see the face of "the Man in the Iron Mask."

The Mask spent half of his life in prison. Five years before the Mask's death, the new governor of the **Bastille** moved him from a prison on the island of Sainte-Marguerite to the Bastille. During the trip, the Mask traveled with curtains hanging all around him.

When the governor and the Mask stopped at a country inn to eat, the innkeeper caught a glimpse of the masked man. But he did not see his face. The prisoner always had his mask on. The governor guarded the Mask carefully. The governor had two pistols. He kept them on the table ready to fire if he needed them.

The man's mask, by the way, was not actually made of iron. It was made of black velvet fabric. The myth of an iron mask comes from the French writer **Voltaire**.

Voltaire's poetry criticized the government and religion of his time. He went to prison because of his ideas. Voltaire was a prisoner in the Bastille in 1717. The Mask had died in the Bastille years earlier.

Over a period of 34 years, the Mask was held in four different prisons, including the Bastille.

While he was in the Bastille, Voltaire talked to people who had seen the Mask. He learned that the Mask was tall and had good manners. The Mask was treated with great respect. He could have anything he asked for except his freedom. The Mask's true identity was a **state secret**. The few people who knew who he was were sworn to secrecy. They vowed never to tell anyone the truth. Voltaire decided that the mystery man was someone important.

One rumor at the time said that the Mask was the brother of King Louis XIV. The king's father, Louis XIII, had a chief minister named Cardinal Richelieu. When Richelieu wrote the story of his own life, he said that Louis XIV had a twin brother. Louis XIV was the first-born son. This meant he was in line to become king of France. Richelieu said the other son was sent off to England. This was so he would not grow up and claim he had a right to be king.

If the younger son did return to France, it seemed likely he would be locked up somewhere. That would keep him from claiming the throne. No one would be allowed to see his face, so no one would notice that he looked like King Louis XIV.

In 1850, French author Alexandre Dumas wrote about the theory that King Louis XIV had a twin who was hidden behind an iron mask. The story was part of his historical novel *The Viscount of Bragelonne*.

Another theory is that the Mask might have been a man called Eustache Dauger. He was sent to a prison in Italy in 1669. A Frenchman named Saint-Mars ran the prison. Saint-Mars received a letter instructing him to guard the prisoner closely. However, he was told not to listen to anything the prisoner said. In fact, he was told to threaten to kill the prisoner if he talked about anything other than his basic needs. At the same time, though, Saint-Mars was told to treat the prisoner with respect. According to this story, the man was not forced to wear a mask, but he was kept apart from other prisoners.

This sounds much like the mysterious masked man who traveled to the Bastille 30 years later. In fact, the governor who guarded the masked man on the trip was Saint-Mars.

In 1930, a French historian found references to a man named Eustache Dauger. This man lived at the same time as King Louis XIV and was about the same age. Eustache's father, François, was the captain of the guard for Cardinal Richelieu. Some people believe François was the real father of Louis XIV.

This painting shows Queen Anne with a child. The child looks like a girl but is actually the future King Louis XIV.

Louis XIV's parents were Queen Anne and King Louis XIII. They had been married for 22 years without having children. Louis XIII was often ill. Everyone had given up hope that the king and queen would have a child. When Queen Anne gave birth to a son in 1638, many people were surprised. The baby did not look like the king. The baby was strong and healthy. As he grew up, many people noticed that the boy looked like François' son, Eustache Dauger.

If Louis XIV was really Eustache's brother, then he was not the true son of Louis XIII. In order to protect his own claim to the throne, Louis XIV would want to keep Eustache Dauger hidden away. The mask would make sure no one noticed that Eustache looked like the king.

Was the Mask Eustache Dauger? Was Eustache the king's brother? No one knows for sure. ✳

CHAPTER THREE
The Dauphin

Louis-Charles, the dauphin, was so good-natured that even the prison guards were impressed with him.

In 1792, the **French Revolution** brought an end to the monarchy. France no longer had a king. The leaders of the new government executed King Louis XVI and his wife. Their two children, Louis-Charles and Marie-Thérèse, were put in prison. They were kept in the Temple, a **medieval** fortress. Louis-Charles was the **dauphin**, the oldest son of a French king. But he was not treated as royalty. He had a tutor who was often cruel. However, the tutor's wife seemed to genuinely care for the boy.

In January 1794, the tutor and his wife were told they would no longer be taking care of the boy. Louis-Charles was moved to a dark, damp cell. For more than a year, he wasted away. By the time a doctor was called, the boy was very sick.

The doctor suggested he should be moved to the country. Fresh air might help him get well.

The authorities ignored the doctor's suggestions. Soon afterward, the doctor became ill and died. Friends suspected he had been poisoned because he knew something the authorities did not want others to find out. For example, perhaps the boy in the cell was not really the dauphin.

In June 1795, another doctor was called to the boy's cell. In the bed, the doctor found the dead body of a ten-year-old boy. The authorities told the doctor the boy was Louis-Charles. The doctor reported that he had died of **tuberculosis**.

When the people of France found out the dauphin had died, many did not believe it. Two years later, police in northeastern France found a boy wandering the streets. He claimed he was the lost dauphin. A number of people believed him, including a guard from the Temple prison. The boy stuck to his story until he died in 1812.

In 1814, the wife of the dauphin's tutor made a startling claim. She said that she had helped smuggle the dauphin out of the prison. In his place, she left a very sick child. This child was the one found dead of tuberculosis, not the dauphin.

This claim opened the door for a string of pretenders. They came from countries all over the world. The most believable pretender turned up 38 years after Louis-Charles was declared dead. Karl Wilhelm Naundorff was a clock maker from Prussia. When he arrived in Paris in 1833, he knew many details about the royal family. Some people who knew the royal family believed he was the son of King Louis XVI. However, Marie-Thérèse, the dauphin's sister, refused to believe the claim.

Naundorff tried to take his case to court. Instead he was arrested and sentenced to prison. He died in 1845, still claiming to be the king's son. Some suspected he had been poisoned.

For the next 150 years, scholars and scientists tried to figure out the truth about the dauphin's death. In 1894, the coffin that held the body of the boy who died in prison was dug up. Scientists decided that the body was that of an older child, not the king's son.

In the 1940s, a historian examined samples of Naundorff's hair. He compared the samples with hair that had come from Louis-Charles. He declared them nearly identical. But that is not the end of the story.

When the boy in the cell died in 1795, the doctor performed an **autopsy** and took out the boy's heart. The heart was still available in 2000. By then, scientists understood how DNA could help confirm a person's identity.

Laboratories compared DNA in samples from the heart with DNA from the hair of Louis-Charles's mother. The results showed the two were related. But DNA testing cannot prove for sure that the heart belonged to the queen's son.

DNA studies also show that it is unlikely that Karl Naundorff was the queen's son. What became of the boy who would have been king of France? The truth remains uncertain.

Karl Wilhelm Naundorff claimed that he was the dauphin. He said he was drugged, placed in a coffin, and rescued on the way to the graveyard.

CHAPTER FOUR

The Duchess

Although she looks serious in this photograph, Grand Duchess Anastasia was usually outgoing.

Russian history changed forever in March 1917. This was the year of the **Russian Revolution**. The revolutionary army forced **Tsar** Nicholas II from the throne. Nicholas II was the last of the Romanov tsars. The **Bolsheviks** took over the rule of Russia. The next year, the Bolsheviks sent Nicholas II and his family to a house in Ekaterinburg.

Nicholas and his wife, Alexandra, had four daughters, Olga, Tatiana, Marie, and Anastasia, and a son, Alexei. Crown prince Alexei had **hemophilia**. This disease prevents the blood from clotting properly. The youngest daughter, Grand Duchess Anastasia, was the family clown.

The family moved to Ekaterinburg with servants and the royal physician. A few months later, the pro-tsarist

White Army closed in on the tsar's house. They wanted to rescue the royal family.

The Bolsheviks could not allow a rescue to happen. They gathered the Romanovs, their servants, and the doctor in a small room. Then the guards opened fire on them.

The guards loaded the victims onto a truck. At least one daughter had survived the attack because she cried out as the guards carried her. The guards drove to the forest and dug a mass grave. They threw the bodies in.

The Bolsheviks put up notices saying the tsar had been executed. They said the rest of the family had been sent to a safe place. Because of this, many people believed the royal family was still alive. Pretenders began to come forward. They claimed to be members of the family.

The Russian royal family. Seated from left: Olga, Nicholas, Anastasia, Alexei, Tatiana. Standing from left: Marie, Alexandra.

A year after the execution, a boy said he was Alexei. Later he admitted he was not. In 1927, another young man claimed to be Alexei. This man had hemophilia, the same disease Alexei had. In 1949, a prisoner in a Russian labor camp convinced doctors he was Alexei. He seemed to know a lot about the tsar's palace. In the end, though, the doctors sent the man back to the camp. In 1960, a Polish spy insisted he was Alexei. He said the whole family had been rescued. Two women said they were his sisters Grand Duchess Olga and Grand Duchess Tatiana.

In 1963, a woman in Illinois published a book claiming she was the tsar's youngest daughter, Anastasia. Few people believed this claim, though, because another woman had a more likely story.

In 1920, a mysterious young woman was pulled from a canal in Berlin, Germany. For a long time, she refused to identify herself. However, one day someone noticed how much she resembled Tatiana, daughter of the tsar. Eventually the woman admitted she was Tatiana's sister Anastasia.

The woman called herself Anna Tchaikovsky. She claimed she had survived the execution and been left for dead. A Bolshevik guard rescued her and married her. When he was killed, she threw herself into the canal in despair.

The children of the Romanov family doctor were certain that Anna was the tsar's daughter. Relatives did not know what to believe. One relative made a list of 18 questions. He thought only the real Anastasia would know the answers. Anna answered all 18 questions correctly. However, another relative uncovered evidence that Anna was really a missing Polish factory worker. The factory worker's brother saw a resemblance, but not enough to be sure Anna was his sister.

By 1928, newspapers and magazines were taking an interest in Anna. One article accused her of being a Romanian actress hired to pretend she was the duchess. Anna began using the name Anna Anderson to protect her privacy.

In 1938, Anna Anderson tried to have her claim legally recognized. The court case dragged on for 29 years. Anna's lawyers presented strong evidence. A scientist showed how closely the measurements of her face matched Anastasia's. Anna had a scar in the same spot where Anastasia once had a mole removed. Both women had similar deformities of the feet. A handwriting expert found 137 characteristics that matched between their handwriting.

A friend said that Anna Anderson's gaze drew people immediately to her.

Despite all this evidence, in 1967 the court ruled that it was not enough. The next year, Anna Anderson moved to the United States. She married Jack Manahan, a retired history professor. On February 12, 1984, Anna died of pneumonia. The mystery that surrounded her would live on.

In 1992, scientists from Russia and the United States announced they had discovered the truth about the Romanov family. They had just finished examining nine skeletons found in a forest near Ekaterinburg. The team used a variety of scientific techniques. These included DNA matching, dental records, and comparing skulls with photographs.

The scientists concluded they had found the skeletons of Nicholas, Alexandra, Olga, Tatiana, and Marie. The other bones belonged to three servants and the royal physician. Scientists had no clues about what happened to Alexei and Anastasia. Perhaps Anna Anderson really was Anastasia.

Scientists got a sample of Anna Anderson's tissue. This came from a hospital that had performed an operation on her. Scientists compared Anna's DNA to that of England's Prince Phillip. Phillip was a relative of Anastasia's mother. They also compared Anna's DNA with that of the great-nephew of the missing Polish factory worker. The tests showed that Anna was related to the factory worker. Scientists did not believe she was related to Prince Phillip. That meant she was not Anastasia.

Some people refuse to accept these findings. Could Anna really be Anastasia? If Anna were alive today, she would probably say what she once said: "You believe it or you don't believe it. It doesn't matter." ✖

CHAPTER FIVE

The Outlaw

This hand-colored photograph is the only known likeness of the outlaw Billy the Kid.

It is easy to understand why someone might claim to be a long-lost prince or princess, but who would want to claim to be the outlaw Billy the Kid? A man named Brushy Bill Roberts did.

No one is sure when Billy the Kid was born, or even what his true name was. Most historians think he was born in New York City. They think he was born around 1859, though no one is sure of the exact year. They also believe his mother was named Catherine Bonney. The Kid was calling himself Billy Bonney when he was 18 years old.

In the middle of the nineteenth century, outlaws roamed the western parts of the United States. Often they traveled in gangs and carried guns. They made their living by stealing cattle and other items.

Billy fought in a dispute between New Mexico ranchers known as the Lincoln County War. Legend says Billy killed a number of men in his outlaw years. In 1880, Billy was convicted of murder. He was sentenced to death by hanging, but somehow Billy escaped.

What happened to Billy the Kid after that seems uncertain. Authorities offered a reward for his capture. By most accounts, Billy died the next year. He was 21 when Sheriff Pat Garrett shot him. The story says that Billy was killed at the house of a friend, Pete Maxwell. Around midnight, Billy came by to carve a steak from a side of beef hanging on the porch. He sensed something was wrong and asked Pete who else was there. That is when Garrett shot Billy the Kid. But even Garrett was not sure he had killed the right man. He did not collect the reward.

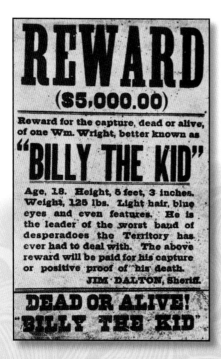

REWARD
($5,000.00)
Reward for the capture, dead or alive, of one Wm. Wright, better known as
"BILLY THE KID"
Age, 18. Height, 5 feet, 3 inches. Weight, 125 lbs. Light hair, blue eyes and even features. He is the leader of the worst band of desperadoes the Territory has ever had to deal with. The above reward will be paid for his capture or positive proof of his death.
JIM DALTON, Sheriff.
DEAD OR ALIVE! "BILLY THE KID"

This reward poster is probably a fake. At age 18, the Kid stood about 5 feet 7 inches tall. The actual reward offered was $500.

Many years later, a new story surfaced. William V. Morrison was an attorney who liked to study history. In 1948, an elderly client named Joe Hines told Morrison that he had fought against Billy the Kid in the Lincoln County War. He said Billy the Kid was still alive.

Morrison decided to find out the truth. His research led him to Brushy Bill Roberts in Hamilton, Texas. Roberts was about 90 years old by this time. At first Roberts denied he was Billy the Kid. Finally he confessed. He was sorry about his early years and all the men he had killed.

As Roberts told his story, Morrison thought Roberts knew a lot of details about Billy the Kid. He must have seen the events for himself. Roberts also answered questions that people had been asking about Billy the Kid for decades.

Roberts claimed he was born William Henry Roberts in Buffalo Gap, Texas, in 1859. When he was three, his mother died. He was sent to live with her half sister, Catherine Bonney. Roberts claimed that Pat Garrett had killed a fellow outlaw, Billy Barlow, at Maxwell's house. The two Billys were about the same size and age. In the dark, they might have looked alike. Roberts said he heard gunshots and ran to investigate. More gunshots followed. Roberts was hit several times, but he was not killed.

Roberts told Morrison that a Mexican woman took him in and tended to his wounds. As soon as he was well enough to travel, he went to Mexico.

Some evidence supports Roberts's story. One deputy claimed that Garrett shot the wrong man. Another deputy said that he, not Garrett, had shot the wrong man. He believed Billy the Kid had gotten away.

It's hard to say what really happened that dark night. However, Brushy Bill Roberts's story was convincing. Morrison believed him. Even as an old man, Roberts looked like Billy the Kid. He was the right age and size. He had the same protruding ears. His hands were small, just like Billy the Kid's had been. Roberts had scars from old bullet wounds in all the right places. His eyes, like the Kid's, were blue-gray with brown spots. Morrison got signed **affidavits** from several other people who believed Brushy Bill Roberts was Billy the Kid, the famous outlaw.

Roberts seemed sorry about his lawless past. He asked the governor of New Mexico for a pardon. In November 1950, Governor Mabry agreed to meet Roberts and discuss a pardon. Roberts expected a private meeting. Instead, he was met by dozens of people. The governor had invited historians, reporters, and police officers. He even invited two of Pat Garrett's sons.

Roberts was elderly and in poor health. He seemed dazed and confused by all the attention. He tried to answer questions, but his answers sounded uncertain. The people listening decided he was just a crazy old man. The governor refused to look at the evidence Morrison had gathered. Roberts returned home ashamed. A month later, he died of a heart attack. It seemed that no one would ever know the truth about Billy the Kid and Brushy Bill Roberts.

Another 40 years passed. In 1990, scientists at the University of Texas at Austin once again considered the identity of Billy the Kid. They used computers to help them. They compared pictures of Roberts with an old **tintype** photograph of the real Billy the Kid. They found that the structure of their faces was amazingly similar. But it was too late for anyone to be sure of the truth. ❋

This is the notice that appeared in the paper when Brushy Bill Roberts died.

It's End of the Trail for Old Texas Cowboy

Brushy Bill Roberts, familiar figure about Hamilton and Hico, fell dead Wednesday at Hico

while standing in front of the newspaper office there. He was the victim of a heart attack.

Brushy was near 90 and could always be recognized by his cowboy attire— a tan 10-gal. hat with leather band, a fringed buckskin jacket and bandanna kerchief. He had documentary proof of some of the claims he made as an old-time rodeo performer, stage coach guard and Indian fighter. He could always spin you a yarn about the early days when outlaws were the principal inhabitants of the country.

The old cowboy appeared on a nation-wide broadcast in January in support of James Dalton's claim that he was Jesse James. Recently Brushy advanced the claim that he himself was Billy the Kid. Wesley Jones of the Western Auto Store personnel here, said Thursday that a report in Hico stated that an attorney from El Paso would arrive there Thursday to substantiate Brushy's claim to his being the fabulous outlaw of early Texas and New Mexican history.

Brushy was straight as an arrow, looked much younger than his actual age and scorned the use of glasses. He told a reporter not long ago: "I never drink tea, coffee or rotgut liquor. I live on sweet milk, cornbread and turnip greens."

Funeral services had not been arranged late Wednesday. He is survived by his wife.

Glossary

affidavits: Written statements made under oath to tell the truth.

autopsy: The examination of a body after death.

Bastille: A fourteenth-century fortress in Paris used to hold political prisoners. At the beginning of the French Revolution, a crowd stormed the Bastille and set all the prisoners free.

Bolsheviks: One of two groups of the Russian Social Democratic Labor party. The Bolsheviks believed in violent revolution. *Bolshevik* means "majority" in Russian.

dauphin: The eldest son of a French king.

DNA: The genetic material in the cells of humans and other living things. DNA stands for deoxyribonucleic acid.

execution: The act of putting a guilty person to death.

French Revolution: (1789–1799) A violent uprising sparked by food shortages and resentment of the middle class toward the upper class.

hemophilia: A disorder that causes a person's blood not to clot. Even a small cut or bruise can cause excessive bleeding.

Louis XIV: (1638–1715) French king whose reign lasted for 72 years, more than any other monarch in European history.

medieval: Relating to the Middle Ages.

Russian Revolution: A social and political uprising in 1917 that took Tsar Nicholas II out of power. Leaders formed a new government and eventually killed the tsar.

state secret: Information kept secret because it is important to keeping an entire country safe.

theory: An idea that explains something, but is not yet proved.

tintype: An early type of photograph taken on a sheet of iron.

tsar: A ruler of Russia before the Russian Revolution of 1917. Nicholas II was the last tsar, ruling from 1894 to 1917.

tuberculosis: A disease of the lungs.

Voltaire: The pen name of famous French writer François-Marie Arouet (1694–1778). Voltaire criticized the royal rulers, the church, and the justice system.

White Army: Russian forces that opposed the Bolsheviks during the Russian Revolution of 1917.

Find Out More

Books

Blackwood, Gary L. *Outlaws*. New York: Marshall Cavendish, 2001.

This book tells about Billy the Kid and other "bad guys."

Blackwood, Gary L. *Perplexing People*. New York: Marshall Cavendish, 2006.

For readers who would like to learn more about pretenders, this book goes into more detail.

Englar, Mary. *Grand Duchess Anastasia Romanov*. New York: Capstone Press, 2008.

What was it like to live in the Russian royal family? This book provides a view of the daily life of Grand Duchess Anastasia.

Kudlinski, Kathleen V. *Joan of Arc*. New York: Dorling Kindersley, 2008.

This book tells the amazing story of Joan of Arc and is filled with colorful photographs and art.

Movies

Anastasia, **directed by Anatole Litvak.**

This 1956 classic, based on the stage play of the same name, made Anna Anderson into a celebrity.

Joan of Arc, **directed by Christian Duguay.**

This film version of Jeanne d'Arc's career was originally shown on television in 1999.

Website

http://www.royalty.nu

This site is full of facts about royal families of various times and places.

Index

Page numbers for photographs and illustrations are in **boldface**.